P9-EFG-350

The British Empire from photographs

AFRICA

THE
BRITISH EMPIRE
from photographs

AFRICA

John Fabb

B. T. BATSFORD LTD, LONDON

Frontispiece *A travelling party of hunters in South Africa, 1879.*

First published 1987

ISBN 0 7134 5207 2

Typeset and printed in Great Britain
for the publishers
B. T. Batsford Ltd,
4 Fitzhardinge Street
London W1H 0AH
by Butler & Tanner Ltd
Frome and London

INTRODUCTION

Victorian Africa was an exciting land of gold, ivory, slaves and big game. Photographs of British Africa do not appear until the 1850s, and then it was usually South Africa, or Cape Colony, that supplied them. As a sphere of influence, rather than a colony, Egypt does have a place in the history of photography in Africa. Before Egypt came under British sway, images were taken by an English doctor, C. G. Wheelhouse, who toured the area with a leisurely yachting party of titled Englishmen in 1849–50. Wheelhouse brought calotype equipment with him. This was a process invented by Fox Talbot and patented by him in 1841, and was the first practicable negative process on paper. Writing paper was treated with solutions of silver nitrate and potassium iodide and then dried. Just before use this was further sensitized with gallo-nitrate of silver. After exposure of two to three minutes the latent negative image was developed with a second solution of gallo-nitrate of silver, washed and fixed with potassium bromide. All this had to be done under the sweltering African heat, even with the help of servants on the deck of Wheelhouse's yacht. Contact prints were then made on similarly sensitized paper under ordinary daylight. Calotype prints were distinguished by a reddish brown colour and a completely matt surface. The images taken by Wheelhouse were unfortunately destroyed by fire in 1879.

Early photographers

John Shaw Smith—a wealthy Irishman—also visited Egypt and was able to record 300 calotypes in 1852. He was followed in 1857 by Felice Beato on his way to photograph the Indian Mutiny. James Robertson was also working at this period, while superintendent of the Turkish Imperial Mint at Constantinople. Except for the northern and southern tips, Africa was photographically untouched. In the early Victorian period the country was largely inaccessible, exploration and settlement being concentrated on the source of the Nile, Cape Town—at the tip of Africa—and Zanzibar—on the east coast—the stepping off point for exploration inland and the depot for the slave and ivory markets. But it was to the Nile that the early explorers first turned their attentions.

The search for the source of the Nile

The whereabouts of the source of the Nile was a mystery that had intrigued men for centuries. This was solved in 1857, on 3rd August, by John Hanning Speke (*Figure 3*), a young English Army Officer, when he came upon a vast lake which he named Victoria 'after our gracious Queen'. At the time, this discovery was unsupported by scientific evidence. His journey had taken him three years from Zanzibar, the starting point, and he then continued down almost the full length of the 4000-odd mile river Nile. He was also for six months the unwilling guest of King Mutesa of Buganda, a bloody tyrant who executed his people at will and lopped off the ears of children who did not pay attention to his words. In July of 1862 Speke located the point where Lake Victoria emptied into the Nile, but his evidence was still inconclusive. He did not circumnavigate the lake to establish that there were no rivers running into it and his claim was challenged by Sir Richard Burton (*Figure 4*), the celebrated explorer whom he had twice accompanied to Africa.

Their second journey together had brought them, after great difficulties, to Lake Tanganyika, and Burton favoured this lake as the fountain head of the Nile. It was here also, at Karagwe, that Speke saw the royal wives—so fat they could not stand up. One lady had a bust of 52 inches, and was only 5 foot 8 inches tall! When raised to her feet, she fainted. In September of 1864 Burton and Speke were due to debate their opposing views on the source of the Nile, but Speke was killed by his own gun when out shooting birds. The verdict was accidental death, but it was concluded by many that this 37-year-old explorer had committed suicide rather than have his unscientific theories demolished by Burton, who wrote to a friend after the incident: 'The charitable say that he shot himself, the uncharitable say that I shot him'. Cameras were not carried on these expeditions, as the difficulties of the country and the need for more important scientific equipment, food, gifts for native chiefs and weapons precluded their use at this early stage.

Burton and Speke were both Army men, from the Indian forces. Together they had explored Somalia in 1853—a dangerous and hazardous journey. The 42-man party was attacked by hostile tribesmen; one British officer was fatally speared, and Speke was stabbed and received 11 wounds. Burton was also injured and photographs show the scars of this encounter. Over the years he suffered similar injuries in Africa, but died in his bed of natural causes at the age of 70.

The collodion process

It was at this period, in 1851, that Frederick Scott Archer established a process that was to remain the principal method of photography for the next 25 years, superseding the daguerreotype and calotype within a few years. This discovery was the wet plate or wet collodion process, a negative photographic process in which collodion held the sensitizing chemicals on a glass plate. Collodion is a viscous transparent substance which, with soluble iodides and bromides, was poured over a glass plate. This was immediately sensitized with silver nitrate and exposed in the camera while still wet, as the chemicals deteriorated if the collodion was allowed to dry. The latent negative image was developed immediately with pyrogallic acid or ferrous sulphate and then fixed with sodium thiosulphate. The glass negative could thus be used to make prints on albumen paper. Free of any patent, the wet plate expanded photography a great deal. It was also the fastest process of its time, with exposures of ten seconds, and even less when adapted for instantaneous exposures in stereoscope cameras. There was, of course, one main disadvantage, and that was the need to sensitize, expose and develop the plates all within a very short period of time—a great hindrance to the photographer in Africa who was obliged to transport all the cumbersome equipment with him. This was, however, a popular process and received widespread use until the arrival of the dry plate.

Francis Frith

Francis Frith used the wet plate in Egypt, with all its drawbacks. Entire darkrooms had to be transported up the Nile and across the desert, with boxes of heavy plates, cameras, tripods, jars of distilled water, chemicals and all the accompanying equipment. Developing tents had to be set up within a few steps of the camera. First the negative had to be quickly and evenly coated with the sticky collodion. Then the plate was sensitized, carried to the camera, exposed and taken back to the tent and developed before the collodion dried, as in Africa the collodion dried quickly. Frith recorded his difficulties working amid ether fumes and 130 degrees of heat. '*Now in a smothering tent, with my collodion fizzing, boiling up all over the glass the instant that it touched and, again, pushing my way backwards upon my hands and knees into a slimy rock tomb to manipulate. It is truly marvellous that the results should be presentable at all.*'

The wet plate was more permanent than the paper negative of the calotype. Hundreds of photographs could be printed from a paper negative, but thousands could be printed from collodion glass. The plates were virtually transparent and the clarity and detail of prints made were superb. Frith published two volumes of original photographs, each print accompanied by a descriptive text entitled *Egypt and Palestine photographed and described*, in an edition of 2000 copies. This was so popular that Frith made a second journey to Egypt in 1859 and sailed up the Nile to the second cataract and continued by camel beyond the fifth cataract. Some of the images he took were published as prints measuring 20 inches by 15 inches. The publicity resulted in the beginnings of tourism, and Egypt became a fashionable country for a Victorian lady to include in her foreign tour. One such lady traveller, Amelia Edwards, found Abu Simbel 'swarming with tourists', and this was in 1873.

Photography was then an expensive pastime, which is why the few genuine amateurs there were in those early days were drawn almost exclusively from the upper middle class. Others made photography a full-time business, such as Frith and Richard Beard. The number of books illustrated with photographs increased considerably at this time.

David Livingstone

European settlements extended only a little way from the coast and were usually trading posts; missionaries, however, penetrated into the heart of the country. The most famous was David Livingstone (*Figure 6*) who was ordained as a member of the London Missionary Society in November of 1841 and a month later embarked for South Africa. During the next ten years he was constantly on the move, up country, in the process gaining fame as an explorer; he was awarded the Royal Geographical Society's Gold Medal for his part in the discovery of Lake Ngami. He suffered a severe mauling by a lion in 1844 and virtually lost the use of his left arm. He was photographed in London in the early 1850s before his departure for Africa again to find a route from east to west that would encourage trade and thus undercut slavery. He set out in 1853 on 11th November equipped with barter goods, six guns and a magic lantern 'to convey the elementary truths of the Bible'. Unfortunately he did not carry a camera. He reached journey's end in March 1856 and published his famous journal, *Missionary Travels*, in 1857, the story of a 4000 mile trek through unexplored country. It sold 70,000 copies and he became a national hero. Returning to Africa in 1858 he embarked on an expedition with a group of missionaries, an unhappy occasion marred by bitterness between the members of the party. In 1865 he began his final attempt to find the source of the Nile, alone, except for his African bearers.

Henry Morton Stanley

Rumours of Livingstone's death abounded. No European had seen him since 1866. It was then that an American newspaper proprietor, James Gordon Bennett, summoned his star reporter—Henry Morton Stanley—to find Livingstone. Stanley (*Figure 7*) was Welsh by birth and had fled to the U.S.A. after an early life in the poor house. He joined the Confederate Army in the Civil war of 1861, was captured at the battle of Shiloh when he changed sides to escape a prison camp, and finally joined the U.S. Navy. In his spare time he wrote stories about the war at sea; these were accepted by various newspapers and he soon became a freelance journalist. In 1868 he joined the *New York Herald* and was summoned to find the hero of Europe and America.

He started for the interior from Zanzibar and bribed or negotiated his way through hostile tribes. The two explorers finally met in November of 1871 at the village of Ujiji. Livingstone was unwell and low on supplies, and wrote of the meeting in his journal: 'But when my spirits were at their lowest ebb, the good Samaritan was at hand.'

Stanley's book, *How I found Livingstone*, was a best seller, published in 1872. He lost the taste for journalism, becoming an explorer and making several important journeys into Central Africa, wearing his well-known white-peaked cap, in which he was often photographed.

The dry plate process

The true beginnings of modern photography came with the introduction of the dry plate, much used by photographers in Africa and in particular by the missionaries. This process was invented in 1871 by Doctor Richard Leach Maddox, an amateur photographer and former doctor of medicine. The process involved coating the photographic plate with gelatin emulsion, instead of wet collodion. The dry plate process was developed further by J. Burgess, who in July of 1873 offered for sale a prepared gelatin for plate making. J. King published a detailed description of this process in 1873 also. Further improvements were made by W. B. Bolton and Richard Kennett. In 1874 Peter Mawdsley founded the Liverpool Dry Plate and Photographic Printing Company, the first to sell dry plates commercially. These ranged in sizes from $4\frac{1}{4}$ inches by $3\frac{1}{4}$ inches up to 12 inches by 10 inches. The great advantage of the dry plate method was that prepared plates could be stored until needed. In Africa this was a tremendous advantage when journeys into the interior could take up to three months. Dry plates also did away with the need for a portable darkroom.

Photographic prints

The prints made from dry plate negatives were albumen and later bromide positives. Albumen prints were invented by L. D. Blanquart-Evrard in 1850 and remained in constant use until well into the 1890s. The majority of positive images produced in Victorian Africa were printed by this method. Albumen paper for photographic positives was prepared with a thin coating of white of egg, which had the effect of smoothing out the irregularities and negating the porosity of the paper. This treated paper unfortunately had a yellowish tinge, which was removed by toning with chloride of gold in hypo, which gave the sepia tint to the positive so typical of Victorian photographs. Carbon prints were invented by Alphonse Louis Poitevin in 1855, but were not satisfactory until improved by Sir Joseph Swann, who produced a ready-made paper which had already been coated with gelatin containing carbon powder. Then a print could be made which, when washed, removed any unexposed and therefore unhardened areas of gelatin, leaving the positive image on the hardened gelatin. Three shades of print were produced on the carbon printing paper, purple, sepia or black, and this was used for reproducing copies.

The hand-held cameras of the late 1870s became more widely used in Africa, and again it was the unknown amateurs who supplied the images that allow us to see Victorian Africa. Cape Colony was the earliest part of the country to receive colonists, and they supplied posterity with many views of ox waggons and weary families on their way north (*Figure 29*).

Lion and elephant were common in those earlier days, and for a time ivory dominated the inland trade. Elephant tusks found ready buyers in London, the world's main distribution centre for this commodity. Hunters made a good living and were able to get six shillings per pound in 1868. These high prices encouraged hunters and traders to extend their operations, and elephants were slaughtered on a scale comparable to the buffalo hunting in the American West.

The hunting of elephants over a wide area also led to the revival in the search for gold. Henry Hartley discovered gold in 1865 when he was hunting an elephant beyond the Limpopo River. By chance the beast fell dead on a quartz reef containing visible traces of gold. In 1869 Sir John Swinburne led a mining expedition to Tati and Thomas Baines led a prospecting expedition to Mashonaland. Baines arrived at a time when the Matebele chieftainship was in dispute, but when Chief Lobengula became paramount chief in 1870 Baines was able to obtain a concession from him. However, Baines soon found himself in financial difficulties as investors would put up no more money to keep the venture going. Apart from collecting much useful information about the country and focusing world attention on the existence of gold in the interior, the expedition accomplished little.

Cecil Rhodes

It was now left to Cecil Rhodes (*Figure 34*), who was head of the de Beers mining company, to secure mining concessions, which he did in 1888, from Lobengula. This led to the occupation of that part of Africa known as Rhodesia. Rhodes was the son of an English vicar; because of poor health when he was a youth he was sent to join his brother in South Africa. He forsook farming to search for his fortune in Kimberley, and by 1888 controlled the whole of the diamond industry. At his own cost Rhodes was able, through the Royal Charter granted to the British South Africa Company, to extend British influence north into Mashonaland and Matebeleland, which in time became North and South Rhodesia and now Zimbabwe. He died in the Cape on 26th March 1902.

Lobengula

Lobengula, paramount Chief of the Matebele, was never photographed as he believed that the camera would take away his spirit. He succeeded his father, Mzilikazi, in 1870. His father was an outstanding Zulu general who broke away from the Zulu kingdom to form his own state in the north. The military despotism of Lobengula could not, however, survive alongside western civilisation, and the inability of the Matebele chiefs to adjust themselves to changing conditions brought tragedy in its train. As a warlike race they felt they had never really been conquered, but were living in mutual trust with the British South Africa Company. Locusts had ravaged the land and this had been followed by rinderpest, which the veterinary officers had tried to stamp out by large-scale slaughter of cattle. The tribesmen could not understand the reason for the destruction of what had been their sole token of wealth. Lobengula also strove for peace, but could not prevail upon the younger chiefs who had not yet made their mark as warriors and who wished to continue raiding in order to build up their status within the tribe. Conflict escalated.

The war of 1893 was disastrous to the Matebele, after several engagements in which Lobengula's Impis fought with desperate gallantry against the unequal power of Maxim machine gun fire. Bulawayo, the capital, was reached, and Lobengula fled, leaving it in ashes. With the news of his death, in January 1894, resistance collapsed.

Cetshwayo

Cetshwayo became King of Zululand in 1872, and he was perhaps the most famous and well-known African leader (*Figure 24*). His was the largest kingdom south of the river Limpopo. He was more intelligent than his Father Mpande, consulted carefully with his counsellors, and was also popular with his people. His first care was to revive the army; conscription was enforced on all the young men, and none of them was allowed to marry before the age of 40. The army was confident and aggressive and looked for action. Towards Natal and South Africa Cetshwayo pursued a conciliatory policy, but after the British occupied the Transvaal in 1877 friction became evident along disputed borders. Various incidents gave the British the opportunity to send an ultimatum to Cetshwayo to disband the Zulu army within 30 days. The British believed that there could be no permanent peace in South Africa until the Zulu kingdom had been destroyed.

The Battle of Isandhlwana

The British force of 7000 regulars and 7000 Natal levies marched into Zululand to attack on 22nd January 1879. They met the 30,000 strong Zulu army at Isandhlwana unexpectedly, and the British lost 1600 men in that disastrous engagement. Photographs of the battlefield taken later show the burnt-out waggons and the bleached skeletons of the soldiers before they were buried.

The end of the war was a foregone conclusion; although the Zulu army had some firearms they were not used to them, so they fought with the same short spear and shield that they had used since the days of their famous King Shaka in the 1820s. After the battle of Ulundi the Zulu army was disbanded. Cetshwayo was captured and banished to Cape Town, and Zululand was divided into 13 territories, each with its own chief. Cetshwayo returned to his country in 1883 and died the next year.

Among the protectorates established by the British, Bechuanaland was set up in 1885 for a number of tribes occupying an area of some 220,000 square miles in Southern Central Africa. Eight tribes were ruled by powerful chiefs who were recognized by the British as representatives of their people. It was through this area that Livingstone travelled during his first missionary exploration visits. These tribal chiefs could trace their ancestors back to the seventeenth century, the most senior, the Bakwena, to the sixteenth century. They were in turn related to the two most senior tribal chieftains in the country, the Bamangwato and the Batawana. The Kalahari desert covers much of this land, but in the Victorian era was teeming with game—rhino, lion and zebra—as well as hosts of ostrich.

West Africa

During the reign of Queen Victoria the British consolidated their hold on the west coast of Africa, which was the first part of darkest Africa to be explored and traded with. It was for many years known as the white man's grave, because of the unpleasant climate.

The Gold Coast colony contained nine kingdoms, the most important being Ashanti. The kings of Ashanti became very powerful in west Africa and resisted the encroachment of the British, but the Gold Coast became a British colony in 1850. There were numerous Ashanti wars, with the war in 1895–96 ending in the capture of King Prempeh and the complete control of the state passing into British hands. The king was photographed with his entourage at the end of the fourth war, on his way to exile (*Figure* 44). The Gold Coast was renowned for its trade and was the earliest point of contact between Europeans and Africans: guns for the Ashanti, gold and black ivory (as slaves were called) for the Europeans.

This part of Africa was not extensively photographed and we have to rely on European missionaries and the army for the little there is available. Most of these photographs date from the late part of the nineteenth century, when the hand-held camera was invented.

George Eastman's films and cameras

In 1881 George Eastman had formed the Eastman Dry Plate Company and in 1884 he introduced the Eastman Negative Paper, using a paper to carry the gelatin emulsion instead of glass. In 1889 Eastman then patented the cellulose transparent film which had been invented by one of his own chemists, Henry M. Reichenbach. Kodak was the name of the camera Eastman invented to carry his film in 1888. One hundred pictures could be exposed at the press of a button, and the film was then processed and developed by the Eastman factory. The whole camera was sent at that time and was returned to the customer complete with a new roll of film, ready to use. This camera was extensively used by missionaries, colonists and the army all over Africa, while professionals favoured the glass plate camera for the excellent results it gave.

Big game hunting

Africa was the sportsman's paradise, as game was abundant. Initially the elephant was shot purely for commercial gain—for its tusks. These were worth a great sum of money and could pay for a safari outright. In Victorian times they ranged from the Cape up to the Niger. In the latter half of the nineteenth century they were protected in the Cape, and a licence, at a cost of £20.00, was required to shoot elephants.

At times it was a dangerous exploit to hunt elephants on foot; a shot through the brain was the only sure way of stopping the huge beasts. To be caught by a wounded elephant was death. Cobus Klopper, a Boer hunter, lost his life when a male elephant came to the aid of a female. The elephant rushed upon him, driving his ivory tusk into his body. He afterwards trampled him beneath his feet, then lifted the body with his trunk and threw the remains into the thorn forest. The largest elephant shot in the Victorian era was recorded at a height of 10 foot 9 inches, in East Africa. The largest tusks were 9 foot 4 inches in length, on an elephant shot by Sir John Kirk.

The rhinoceros was another of the dangerous big game animals popular with the Victorian sportsman. Old hands used to say 'men are the only enemies whom he fears and this fear ceases when he is wounded.' They were found from Abyssinia down to the Cape, alert and active, which made them that much more dangerous. It is recorded that a white hunter at the Cape, a Mr Oswell, was killed when a rhino threw both his horse and himself into the air with one blow of his horn. The Africans hunted them for their meat, which was considered a delicacy, and for the horns, for their supposed aphrodisiac qualities.

The express rifle, with a large charge of powder, was a favoured weapon, usually a .500 bore up to .600 bore. Many used the army version .303 rifle for smaller game or those animals that did not have such a thick skin or heavy horns.

The lion was also a popular trophy and had a wide geographical distribution, from Algeria to the Cape. The largest recorded specimen shot was 10 foot 5 inches long, from South East Africa. The Masai tribe in Kenya Colony have long held the lion in high esteem and it was required that the young men should prove themselves by fighting a lion in single combat, armed only with a spear.

The hunting safari

Countless deer, antelope, gazelle and buck horns and heads adorned the homes of Victorian sportsmen. Elephants' feet were made into footrests and wine coolers, hooves served as inkwells, birds were mounted as firescreens, rhinoceros hide covered trays and tables and animal skins served as rugs, with or without mounted heads displaying a snarling row of teeth. The cost of such expeditions was of course high, and only the rich could afford an African safari, which would involve many months travel on the veldt.

Bearers, guides and a white hunter had to be hired, usually in Zanzibar. Preparations were similar to those of a small military expedition. There would be tents for the members of the party, a dining tent and a skinning tent, tents for, say, 200 porters, gun bearers, tent boys, Askaris—native soldiers—and sometimes horse boys. The porters were chosen from several different tribes or races to minimise the danger of them joining forces in the event of a mutiny. The backbone of such a safari was generally composed of Swahili, coast men who had become Muslims. (It was these Swahili who searched for ivory and slaves for the Arabs before the white explorers arrived.) Two tent boys would look after one man's belongings, wait at table and pull a bath when required after a hot day before dinner (*Figure 48*).

The hunter's wardrobe would consist of hobnail boots, khaki breeches or trousers, the knees faced with leather and the legs buttoning tight from the knee to below the ankle, a khaki shirt, pith helmet and, maybe, sand goggles or sunglasses. Each man would carry such armament as a 30 calibre rifle, a double-barrelled .500 or .450 rifle and a shotgun. In his pockets would be a knife, compass and a waterproof matchbox. The camp would be broken as early in the morning as possible; each bearer had his alloted task, and the tents, provisions and bedding were made into suitable packages for the porters to carry. Each porter handled a load of about 60 lb, and the men would sing on the march or blow on whistles to keep up a rhythm.

On a long journey there would be a break at noon, and then the march would continue until game was found or a camp site chosen. On reaching the camping ground each man would at once set about his allotted task; tents were quickly pitched, water and fuel were fetched. The tents would be pitched in a long line; first would be the accommodation of the white hunters, then the dining tent. In another line would be the cook's tent, the provision and store tents. The porters would sleep in the open around camp fires. If suitable game was found breakfast would be at dawn and a return to the camp would be made for luncheon, otherwise the hunters would be gone all day.

Medicines and provisions
The problem of health was always prevalent; far from any medical help, an expedition for hunting or exploration needed to carry a medical kit. This would consist of quinine, spirits of nitre, chlorodyne, ipecacuanha, Warburgh's tincture, laudanum, castor oil (a good Victorian standby), iodoform (for ulcers and sores), powdered sulphur for 'itch'—a common and disagreeable complaint—and a good cough mixture in concentrated form. All this would need to be brought out from England, as well as other comforts such as soups, champagne, brandy and port wine.

Provisions for the safari would include potted meats in small tins, salt, mustard, pepper, Worcestershire sauce, baking powder, oatmeal, tapioca, sago, pearl barley, essence of lemons for puddings, tea, coffee, cocoa, sugar, candles and whisky. It was also recommended that a few pint bottles of champagne be taken, to be used medically. 'As few things are more efficacious in pulling a man together in cases of extreme prostration after fever or when exhausted from violent exertion, a tumbler of champagne with a teaspoon of brandy in it has a marvellous effect', said one big game hunter. He did add, however, that this remedy should be used in moderation in a climate such as East Africa, and not until the sun was down. 'Providing a man can eat well, stimulants are not necessary', but he added 'a stiff whisky with five grains of quinine on arrival in camp and before having a bath will be found to be a capital pick-me-up and will enable a man to eat, as well as render him unlikely to fall to an attack of fever'.

Boxes carried by the bearers were made with a lock and key, fastened with brass screws and a careful invoice taken of the contents. To prevent the constant opening of the boxes day after day, two or three were kept for general use, stocked with such things as tea, coffee, candles, cocoa, sugar, milk and, of course, a bottle of whisky. These boxes were then refilled from the others as required. On a trip of six months the bearers demanded three months' pay in advance. If the country was dangerous at least 25 of the men would be armed with breach loading rifles, more if they were travelling to the Suk country in Northern Kenya.

The gun bearers, whose job was to carry the hunters' rifles, were not in short supply. Any number of the men would jump at the chance because they preferred to carry the rifle and cartridge bag—some 25 lb—rather than a full bearer's load of about 65 lb. They were also entitled to the heart and liver of any game shot, as part of their perks.

The hunters
His Royal Highness The Duke of Connaught and Strathearn, Major Lord John Cavendish, His Highness the Maharajah of Cooch-Behar and Frank Baden-Powell, brother of the famous Lord Robert Baden-Powell, were among the distinguished British hunters. The most famous American big game hunter was President Teddy Roosevelt (*Figure 78*), who visited Africa with his son and collected a large number of trophies for the museums back in the United States of America.

The greatest white hunter, in the tradition of Alan Quartermain, would possibly be Frederick Courtney Selous. He was a professional hunter, and spent his time from 1871 leading expeditions and hunting big game. He explored Mashonaland, unknown territory which later became the port of Rhodesia, and scouted routes for Cecil Rhodes' various projects. He wrote two books on his adventures in Africa, and when the First World War broke out he joined up at the age of 62. Unfortunately he was killed in action in 1917. A Rhodesian regiment was named in his memory—the crack Selous Scouts.

The earliest wars of the photographic period in Africa were those at the Cape. There were several native uprisings in 1850, 1851 and 1852; competition for land between the Bantus and the settlers advancing north was the cause. These were known as the Kaffir wars. The vague frontier to the north of Cape Colony was known as Kaffraria—the land of the Kaffirs. Kaffir was originally an Arab word for an infidel, and was a term used by the colonists for the Bantus as a whole. There was now peace in this area until the Zulu war of 1879.

Trouble in Abyssinia

To the north another war was fought, though not strictly in the British sphere of influence, in Abyssinia. A British diplomat, Captain Charles Cameron, late of the Indian army, was sent by Her Majesty's Government to the Court of the Emperor Theodore of Abyssinia. He brought with him gifts from Queen Victoria, and the Emperor lost no time in writing his thanks to the Queen and advising her of his intention of sending a delegation to London. Unfortunately the Foreign Office overlooked his request and did not reply to the Emperor's letter. As months passed the Emperor's resentment mounted; he was unfortunately a little insane and began to imagine a conspiracy against him. In 1864 he detained Cameron and his staff and eventually all the Europeans in Abyssinia were imprisoned. By the time further letters, gifts and requests for the release of the Europeans had passed, it was now 1866. British agents sent to intercede were also seized and sent to the fortress capital of Magdala.

It was now obvious that the prisoners would not be released except by force, and the army was got ready to march into Abyssinia and release the prisoners. This force was under the command of General Sir Charles Napier, and landed on the Red Sea coast at Zula, on Egyptian territory. At this time little was known about this part of Africa and scarcely anyone had visited the interior of Abyssinia. Twelve thousand troops assembled at Zula, with 20,000 baggage animals. Half a million pounds sterling in gold coin was taken, the only currency universally accepted in Abyssinia. Three hospital ships floated in the harbour and the Royal Navy also supplied three condensers to produce fresh water. Batteries of artillery were loaded as well as 4000 Snider Enfield rifles for the British troops. The newly formed 10th Company Royal Engineers had with them a team of nine photographers, the first time official photographers were present on a campaign. It carried two cameras so constructed that they could be loaded on mules, together with various lenses and plates. Official photographs were taken of troops on parade, camps and the country generally, and permission was granted for officers to purchase copy prints if they wanted to.

Local princes who were at odds with the Emperor Theodore were coerced into being allies. One of them, Prince Kassai of Tigre, met the

British forces at the river Diab. Gifts were exchanged, toasts drunk and a group photograph taken. First contact with the Emperor's forces was made at the Arogi Pass. Sustained fire by the British breech-loading rifles from disciplined British and Indian Army troops soon broke the wild Abyssinians. It was followed by bayonet charges which ended the battle and left nearly 2000 dead and wounded Abyssinians on the field.

At Magdala the Emperor released the hostages but would not surrender. General Napier decided that the fortress would have to be stormed. Heavy artillery fire and a direct assault on the fortress by the British soon resulted in the capture of Magdala. The Emperor was found dead inside; at the moment when it was clear all was lost he shot himself with a pistol—a gift from Queen Victoria. The British found many prisoners inside, including no less than 36 Abyssinian princes—some of whom had been incarcerated for as many as 30 years.

After two days General Napier ordered the return to Zula; this had been a successful campaign, with British losses of only 35.

Nigeria was originally the home of a British trading empire called The Royal Niger Company, where the army's main task was keeping the French at a distance as they were always ready to encroach on the northern borders. Slave trading was stopped when the Emirs of Nupe and Ilorin came under British influence.

Back in the south of Africa the Zulu War occupied the British army during 1879. Many photographs are available of this campaign and include not only the British troops and their colonial allies but also the Zulus. These images were taken with the dry plate cameras. On a campaign of this style, well away from civilization, the plates could be kept after exposure for development later. By the end of 1879 there were more than 14 companies producing dry plates. Smaller cameras were also manufactured that could be used without a tripod, although they were still a little cumbersome.

Independence for Transvaal

The war in Zululand ended independent native statehood in South Africa, but there was a white minority who had visions of independence, in particular the Transvaal, taken over by the British in 1877 as a bankrupt state, who wanted to follow the example of the Orange Free State.

In December 1880 they proclaimed themselves an Independent Republic. The British sent a regiment from Natal to Pretoria, and as the Connaught Rangers marched behind their band they were shot to pieces by Boer riflemen. Within a few minutes half the regiment were dead or wounded, and a war began.

Another disaster struck the British at Laing's Nek, with the death of 150 men. The Boers would not stand up and fight, but used guerilla tactics and were expert marksmen. The final battle at Majuba Hill was another British disaster, and even the General died on the field (*Figure 34*). Negotiations, concluded in 1881, resulted in Transvaal's independence, but retained for Britain a vague control over the country's foreign affairs. Photographs from this war are limited again to views and groups—mainly due to the short duration of the war and the fact that nobody wished to record a defeat.

In the north of Africa there was more work for the photographers amongst the sand, heat and dust of Egypt and the Sudan. In 1880 an Egyptian Colonel, Ahmed Arabi Bey, had led a revolt against the way the army was maintained. It was badly led by Turkish senior officers, wretchedly dressed, ill fed, and only occasionally paid. He led a group of Egyptian officers to demand the dismissal of the War Minister; although this was granted, little improvement was made. By 1882 the British and French governments were worried over the control of the Suez Canal and the rise to power of Arabi, who was now War Minister. They sent warships to Alexandria to protect the 90,000-strong European population, and demanded the dismissal of Arabi. The Egyptians began to strengthen the defences of Alexandria, while the population rioted, killing and looting foreign businesses. On 11th August 1882 the Royal Navy bombarded the fortresses of Alexandria, reducing them to rubble. Photographs taken three days later show Royal Navy sailors (*Figure 35*) inspecting the ruins. Arabi withdrew his Egyptian army, leaving Alexandria in flames, with mobs roaming the streets. The British soon captured the Suez Canal and, after two battles, at Kassassin and Tel-el-Kebir, Arabi was beaten and surrendered. Photographs taken of this campaign are interesting as they show the last of the red-coated British soldier and the transition into Khaki.

South of Egypt, in the Sudan, the Victorians were soon to lose one of their greatest heroes, General Gordon. The Sudan was a dominion of Egypt, conquered over the years, until by 1870 the southernmost limits had been fixed in equatorial Africa above Uganda and Abyssinia. The rise of the Mahdi in the Sudan as a prophet—The Expected One—had led to the collapse and defeat of the Egyptian Army at Fashoda and the massacre of a whole army under Hicks Pasha in the desert beyond El Obeid. The British advised Egypt to evacuate the Sudan, to which they reluctantly agreed. However, various garrisons were cut off, including Khartoum, with 6000 troops. General Gordon, who had been Governor General of the Sudan in 1877–79 and Governor of the Sudan Equatorial Province in 1874, was sent to assess the situation and report back. He arrived at Khartoum to a rapturous reception, freed all the prisoners, improved the food supply and destroyed the official Egyptian debt records. Photographs of Gordon at this time, the last ever taken, show him in the gold-embroidered uniform as Governor General of the Sudan. Khartoum was then besieged by the Mahdi, but Gordon's relief column came too late, and he died at the hands of the Mahdi hordes, as did all the inhabitants of Khartoum.

At the same time a British force had landed at Suakin on the Red Sea to crush Osman Dinga—a slave trader who had thrown in his lot with the Mahdi. Photographing this particular campaign is interesting as, once again, the 10th Company Royal Engineers were sent from Chatham with their equipment. The photographic team consisted of one N.C.O. and six men. The equipment devised for active service was stored and transported in a waggon fitted up as a darkroom, and they carried two cameras—one taking a picture 12 inches by 10 inches and the other 8 inches by 5 inches. Six lenses were carried, one wide angle, one rapid rectilinear for copying maps, and one single view for each camera.

The British leave the Sudan

British Army successes in this campaign were brought to a halt when the politicians in London decided on complete evacuation of the Sudan. This was carried out in 1898 by General Sir Herbert Kitchener with the Anglo-Egyptian army, a reformed Egyptian army, well trained and disciplined and formed with the British to crush the Mahdi's forces at Omdurman on 2nd September 1898. Photographs depict the 10,000 killed and wounded dervishes after five hours of fighting. Gordon was avenged, and General Kitchener emerged as the hero who had saved British honour in the field, something he would have to do again in a few years against the Boers.

The Boer War 1899–1902

The Boer War was the last great conflict of the empire in Africa. By this time photographs could be reproduced in newspapers and magazines and the output was prolific.

At first the British forces did not do well in the field and suffered three major defeats in one week, the generals and staff being at fault, not the army. The government acted quickly and appointed Field Marshal Lord Roberts as Supreme Commander. Lord Roberts' only son had died just previously at the battle of Colenso, trying to save the guns and winning for himself the Victoria Cross for his supreme sacrifice. By June 1900 Lord Roberts had won control of all the main cities of the Transvaal and Orange Free State. Believing he had won the war he returned to England in triumph.

The Boers, however, were not beaten and moved freely over the country. A new Commander in Chief was appointed—Lord Kitchener. His system of controlling the Boers was to build block houses and criss-cross the country with wire fences, and captured Boers were concentrated into large camps. Politicians at home began to query the way the war was being fought, but Kitchener was unrepentant and a negotiated peace was formulated and signed on 31st May 1902. The Boers did not do so badly under the treaty; Dutch was taught in schools and used in the law courts. Transvaal became a self-governing colony in 1906 and the Orange Free State in 1907. Cape Province and Natal joined the other Provinces in 1910 to become the Union of South Africa. Nationalism did not die and the British, having won the war, lost the peace. The bitterness of the Boers towards the British continued, although this did not stop South Africa supporting the allied cause during the two World Wars.

The Royal Tour of 1947 was enthusiastically received, but republican sympathies prevailed, and the Republic was declared in 1961. Curiously, the flag was not altered, as is the usual case, but continued to be the one flown since 1928.

The First World War broke the German colonial empire in Africa, and some parts were then administered by the British.

The Commonwealth and after

British Africa did not change very much between the World Wars. Education, missionary work and medical aid were expanded, and with education came an awareness of their heritage and a wish for freedom. The African regiments fought well and hard in the Second World War, and with the end of that conflict came thoughts of independence.

The first black African country to become an independent member of the British Commonwealth was the Gold Coast in 1957, and the name was changed to Ghana. Throughout the sixties the Empire was dismembered. All became Commonwealth members except the Sudan, which was administered by Egypt as well; it chose independence instead of joining Egypt. British Somaliland joined Italian East Africa and French Somaliland, and became the Republic of Somaliland. The Empire was now replaced by independent countries.

All retained links with the British, particularly in language, style of government and the armed forces. Unfortunately, the false borders imposed by the European powers in the nineteenth century along lines of latitude and longitude have caused frictions, and domination by one race or tribe over others is common where European borders encompass several tribal areas. With the growth of rights in South Africa for non-whites it will be ironic if, as predicted by some, the Zulu nation dominates that country once again.

BRITISH AFRICAN EMPIRE

Name as part of the British Empire	*Date when granted independence*	*New name where different*
Basutoland	1966	Lesotho
Botswana	1966	Bechunaland
The Gambia	1965	
Gold Coast	1957	Ghana
Kenya	1963	
Nigeria	1960	
Nyasaland	1964	Malawi
Northern Rhodesia	1964	Zambia
Southern Rhodesia		Zimbabwe
Sierra Leone	1961	
British Somaliland	1960	part of Somaliland
South Africa	1928	
Sudan	1956	
Swaziland	1967	
Tanganyika	1964	Tanzania
Uganda	1962	

1 The fallen statue of Ramesses II at Thebes, Egypt 1857. A group of English tourists visiting the site. Egypt, although not a part of the British Empire, was a 'sphere of influence', because of the Suez Canal, the short route to India. The ruins of Egypt were a popular subject for Victorian photographers in the first half of the nineteenth century. The lady rides a donkey and some of the gentlemen carry rifles—possibly to shoot crocodile, numerous at this period on the Nile.

2 *Right* Sir Samuel Baker, 1821–1893. Explorer, hunter, adventurer, soldier of fortune, he arrived in Africa in 1861 together with his wife, and spent sixteen months exploring the tributaries that flowed from Abyssinia into the Nile. In 1864 he discovered Lake Albert, 'an imperishable memorial of one loved and mourned by our gracious Queen'. On their return journey they also discovered the magnificent waterfall which Baker named Murchison Falls, after Sir Roderick Murchison, President of the Royal Geographical Society.

3 *Right* John Hanning Speke. The English army officer and African explorer who found the source of the Nile on 3rd August 1857. He had already twice accompanied Richard Burton on expeditions in Africa. It was on the second of these expeditions that Speke had discovered Lake Victoria. In September 1864 Burton and Speke were due to debate in public their divergent theories on the source of the Nile, but on the eve of the debate Speke shot himself when out shooting birds. He was only 37 years old, and it is unknown if this was an accident or suicide.

4 *Far right* Sir Richard Burton, 1821–1890. He was an army officer and a man of action; he could speak 25 languages, and travelled in the Near East and Africa. His companion on the original expedition to search for the Nile's source was John Speke. However, they argued fiercely and bitterly, and on the death of Speke, Burton wrote: 'the charitable say that he shot himself, the uncharitable say that I shot him'. Burton died in 1890.

5 Group of gentlemen at Cape Town, 1868. Behind them rises Table Mountain. The city itself was one of the more agreeable outposts of the Empire. The climate was not too harsh, there were theatres, some hotels that catered for India's army officers on leave, and despite the clouds of red dust which whirled around, the settlers found the Cape a pleasant spot.

6 Dr David Livingstone, 1813–1873. The famous missionary and African explorer, born at Blantyre, Scotland. In 1840 he landed in South Africa as an ordained member of the London Missionary Society. He explored much of southern Africa and among his discoveries was the Victoria Falls. He fell out with the Boers and the Arabs because of the stand he took against the slave trade. In 1865 he began his final expedition in an attempt to discover the source of the Nile. In 1871 Livingstone was sick and weak and was resting at Ujiji when a large caravan marched into the village headed by his rescuer, Henry Morton Stanley. However, Livingstone died two months later and his devoted servants made a nine month journey to the coast with his embalmed body. It was laid to rest in Westminster Abbey on 18th April 1874.

7 Sir Henry Morton Stanley, 1841–1904. Born in Wales, he sought a new life in the U.S.A. in 1859. Stanley enlisted in the Confederate Army during the American Civil War, and was captured and joined the U.S. Navy to escape imprisonment. In 1868 he joined the *New York Herald* as a reporter, and was given the task by James Gordon Bennett of finding Livingstone. He found him in November 1871 at Lake Victoria. He returned to take up British nationality and was knighted, becoming a Member of Parliament. He later made a fortune in the Belgian Congo.

8 Brigadier Schneider and Staff, Abyssinian War, 1868. This war was caused by the imprisonment of various diplomatic Europeans and missionaries by the insane Emperor Theadore. A force under Sir Charles Napier consisting of 12,000 troops led the attack and, after several battles, the capital Magdala was reached and captured. The battle ended in victory for the British. The emperor refused to surrender and shot himself with a revolver. The British released prisoners including some Abyssinian princes who had been incarcerated for 30 years.

9 At the club, Port Elizabeth, South Africa *c.* 1870. There is little to show that the scene is set in Africa except, perhaps, for the 'stoop' or verandah-type building. The club was a place to sit in the cool of the evening. Seven army officers from the 86th Royal County Down regiment are in the photograph. They were stationed here from 1870–75. A detachment was sent to Natal during disturbances in 1873.

86

10 Dead hippopotamus with hunters *c.* 1870. These large animals were killed by the native population for meat, and any explorer or hunter looking for bearers and guides would oblige with shooting a few of these 'river pigs'. The best way to kill the beast was through the nostril which leads to the brain, when stricken the beast sinks in the water and it may be an hour or two before the carcass rises, depending on the temperature of the water. Hippos were common on all the rivers of Africa from the Nile downwards, but not a popular trophy with Europeans. This is probably Lake Victoria which at this time teemed with animal life.

11 South Africa, Cape Province, 1871. A quiet scene possibly in the cool of late afternoon. The European dress shows considerable affluence and makes no concession to the African heat. The people could be in England except for the fact that the buildings in the background have tin roofs and verandahs. On the right there are two buildings with second floor verandahs, examples of which can still be seen today in parts of Cape Town. There is a notable absence of black Africans in this picture.

12 Armed settlers, South Africa, 1871. This group of settlers and friendly natives from Cape Colony were to help and hinder the regular British Army against native tribes. Small wars continued throughout the nineteenth century as settlers increased their holdings, thereby squeezing the native population north or into the poor mountainous districts.

13 *Above* The Barouche of Cetshwayo, King of Zululand, 1873. It was purchased for his coronation in Durban with four grays by John Dunn, an English settler in Zululand and a friend of the king. Cetshwayo had both an English wife and many Zulu wives. At his death he had 49 wives and 116 children mentioned in his will. The young men in the front are preparing a meal.

14 General Sir Garnet Wolseley. The photograph was taken at the time of the Ashanti War of 1873—a brilliant campaign in West Africa, fighting not only a fearsome adversary, but also the intolerable heat and dense jungle. He later fought in the Egyptian War of 1882 and the Sudan Campaign in the attempt to rescue General Gordon. He received the baton of a Field Marshal in 1896.

15 Sir Henry Morton Stanley at Zanzibar, 1887. The great explorer stands with a group of his bearers at the British Agency, many of whom had been with him on his first expedition to search for Dr Livingstone in 1871. He returned in a blaze of publicity, and the book he wrote on his return *How I Found Livingstone*, published in 1872, was an international best seller. He returned to Africa and achieved much as an explorer in Central Africa. The men pictured here were recruited in Zanzibar and were free men. Other bearers would be recruited as the expeditions moved into the interior.

16 *Overleaf* Buffalo hunters, Delagoa Bay Flats, 1879. A group of white hunters and their gun bearers with a Cape buffalo, near Portuguese East Africa. The 'white hunters' are all armed with percussion rifles, that is, one shot, pushed home with a ram rod. A dangerous sport before the days of the magazine rifle or breech loader. In this early period it was also common to hunt on horseback because of the open countryside.

17 *Inset overleaf* 'Witch doctor' and patient, South Africa, *c.* 1879. The 'witch doctor' is on the right, and her patient (left) is in a trance. 'Witch doctors' used natural herbs and commonsense to cure their patients. They could also put the fear of God into their people and held great power and influence over the entire tribe. Life and death was in their hands.

18 Diamond diggers' camp, Bultfontein, Griqualand West, 1879. A family stand by with a good cup of English tea on the table. The canvas houses and waggons are reminiscent of the American West. Bultfontein is on the border close to the Orange Free State and was the site of a diamond mine in 1870. The first diamonds had been discovered on the Orange and Vaal Rivers and by 1869 10,000 claims had been staked, but these were eclipsed by the discoveries at Bultfontein and Dorstontein in 1870.

19 Kimberley Town, 'the diamond fields capital', South Africa, 1879. Kimberley consisted of hundreds of tents and corrugated iron huts. It was a scorching dust bowl in summer and a morass of mud in winter. The population rocketed to 10,000 people at the peak of the diamond boom. It was simply a matter of scooping up fortunes just below the surface, and there were many such finds; e.g. one miner found a 175 carat diamond at the turn of a spade.

20 Gold fields, Eastern Transvaal, South Africa, 1879. Gold was discovered in the 1850s in sufficient amounts to start 'The Fools Rush'. However, it was not until 1886 that the real strike was found. Johannesburg became the wealthiest gold town of all time with the discovery of a 30 mile reef of gold. Within three years the population rose to 40,000—four times greater than the capital, Pretoria.

21 Coal fields at Newcastle, South Africa, 1879. Apart from gold and diamonds, coal was the other great discovery in South Africa. At this time the mining of coal was from the surface and did not need the deep mines familiar today. Before the days of rail, the ox waggon was the only way of transporting the coal needed for industry and the British steam warships at Simonstown on the coast.

22 A party of hunters, South Africa, 1879. The Europeans are from left to right: Mr Sargeaunt of the Colonial Office and his son, Captain Patterson and Mr Cochrane. Captain Patterson and Mr Sargeaunt Junior died on a subsequent visit to Victoria Falls. There was speculation at the time about whether they were killed accidentally or by order of a native chief.

23 Reading the ultimatum to the Zulus, 11th December 1878. John Shepstone, Secretary for Native Affairs, reading the ultimatum sent to the Zulu King by Sir Bartle Frere, Governor of Cape Colony. The unacceptable terms precipitated the Zulu War which began on 4th January 1879 when Lord Chelmsford and the British forces crossed the Tugela River. He had over 16,000 men and 2,000,000 rounds of ammunition. The Zulu King was able to put in the field 50,000 men grouped into 33 regiments. The shields distinguished the different regiments by the colour markings of the cow hide.

24 Cetshwayo, King of Zululand *c.* 1826–1884. Born *c.* 1826 and son of Mpande, he acceded to the throne in 1873. Cetshwayo was taken to England after the Zulu War and his capture following the battle of Ulundi, 4th July 1879. He was restored in January 1883 but died the following year. He was succeeded by his son Dinuzulu, the great-grandfather of the present King of Zululand.

25 *Left* Cetshwayo's brother, 1879. Uhamu was the brother of King Cetshwayo of Zululand *c.* 1880. Friendly to the British and always at odds with the King, he brought 700 warriors onto the side of the British in the Zulu War of 1879. They were used as guides and irregular troops, and he was regarded by the majority of the Zulu people as a deserter and traitor. He is shown outside his kraal with members of his family.

27 Mehlokazulu Ka Sihayo in irons after his capture at the battle of Ulundi, 4th July 1879. One of the incidents that had given the excuse for the Zulu War to be declared was this chief's pursuit into Natal of two of his wives with their lovers. He subsequently executed the two wives in accordance with Zulu law. This caused a protest by the government in Natal. He was sent to Pietermaritzburg but no charges were pressed and he was later released.

26 Natal Kaffirs from Captain Barton's 4th Battalion of the Natal Native Contingent during the Zulu War 1879. Most of the men are armed with the Martini Henry rifle. The European officers stand at the front. The uniform of the native troops consisted of a red rag tied about the head. They did, however, fight throughout the war and were loyal, if only half-hearted allies of the British.

28 Pretoria coach, 1880. Ready for the run to Johannesburg with a ten horse team. A short run, for as the notice says, 'saloon coaches four times daily'. Although mules were more usual, this team is made up of horses. The coach is of the concorde pattern, famous in the U.S.A. The building in the far left background is the famous Rand Club of South Africa.

OF FINEST
PURE TRANSVAAL & OTHER
GREAT VARIETY OF PIPES
TOBACCO
CIGARS
SNUFF
AND FANCY

29 Ox cart, South Africa, 1880. The common mode of transport in South Africa was a waggon drawn by oxen. Waggons were 18 feet long and 6 feet wide, and required between 12 and 18 beasts to draw them. Ten miles a day could be covered, and with 16 hours for resting and grazing it made for slow progress.

30 *Inset* Visit of a doctor to a native village, 1880. The doctor seated in the centre appears to be vaccinating a child, as the others stand in line. Medicine was one of the great benefits that the Europeans brought with them to Africa.

31 Zulu warriors, 1880. Before joining the army, Zulu boys were put into groups of about 100 under a leader who taught them until they reached military age. They were then formed into regiments of boys of the same age group, and from the same area. They were not allowed to marry until the King gave permission and they were then allowed to wear the *Isicoco*, a fibre circlet woven into the hair, which can be seen in the photograph on the men at the back. The colour of the shield denoted the regiment: black shields denoted youths, red married regiments, and white shields for the most senior and the bravest of all.

32 *Above* Zulu family outside their Kraals, 1880. The Zulu tribe was the most powerful race in southern Africa before the war of 1879. The huts are beehive-shaped and built of bent wood covered with rush mats. It was the custom for Zulu girls to wear nothing except a few beads until they were married, then an apron of fringed tanned leather was adopted, sometimes ornamented with small brass bells.

33 *Left* A Zulu hunting party, 1880. Typical of the hunting methods of the native races of Africa, they are armed with spears and clubs, although the man standing to the right is wearing a cartridge belt. As they did not have the advantage of guns, hunting had to be accomplished with great skill in closing in upon the game and then using the spear or club to kill the animal. The men could be away for days at a time and often returned empty handed.

34 Cecil Rhodes with the officers of the 92nd Gordon Highlanders, South Africa, 1881. During the first Boer War, at the Battle of Majuba Hill they suffered losses of 96 men out of the 118 engaged. Bad leadership had given the Boer sharpshooters easy targets and they knew how to use the terrain. Unfortunately when the second Boer War started 18 years later, it was only too apparent that the British had learned no lessons from the earlier war.

35 Egypt 1882, Royal Navy sailors with nine pounder guns after landing at Alexandria. The men are in their shirt sleeves and wear wide brimmed sennet hats, in contrast to the army in their tight red tunics, helmets and leather equipment. The city defences had been bombarded by eight battleships and eleven gun boats, and by late afternoon all defences had been silenced. On the following day Arabi, the Egyptian leader, and his army evacuated the city and moved inland, leaving the city to rioters and looters until the British arrived to restore order.

Genl. Valentine Baker Pacha & Hicks Pacha
and Staff
Cairo 1883 —

36 *Left* General William Hicks Pasha seated on the extreme right with his officers, 1883. He assumed command of the Egyptian Army and in pursuit of the Mahdi into the Sudanese desert, his ill-prepared men had been massacred, Hicks and his European officers fighting gallantly to the end. In the centre sits General Valentine Baker Pasha, Commander of the Egyptian Gendarmerie, who suffered a similar disaster in 1884 at El Teb, where more than two thirds of his troops were killed.

37 Usipebu's wives, 1883. Usipebu was the cousin of King Cetshwayo of Zululand and had commanded a regiment at the disastrous Battle of Isandhlwana. After the defeat of the Zulus, the kingdom was divided up into 13 parts, each with its own chief selected by the British, and one of these territories was ruled by Usipebu. Each chief was required not to raise an army and also to submit to British arbitration in cases of dispute. It was the custom for Zulu warriors not to marry until about the age of 40, by the king's command. Boys and girls were formed into regiments at an early age, and when permission to marry was granted, they would choose from a regiment of girls assigned by the king. It was a capital crime for any of these girls to marry outside the regiment in question.

38 Lt. Francis Lloyd, Grenadier Guards, 1885. This officer wears the uniform worn at the time of the first Sudan War and the advance to try and rescue General Gordon. The brigade of guards called for volunteers to form a household brigade regiment, mounted on camels, which was used with great success. Unfortunately they arrived too late to rescue General Gordon.

39 Commissariat staff officers, Suakin Field Force, 1885. During this campaign photographs were taken by the 10th Company Royal Engineers. These were semi-official and consisted of groups, troops on parade, the camps and surrounding country. The campaign was against Osman Digna, a supporter of the Mahdi, and it was hoped to build a railway from Suakin on the Red Sea into the interior and link up with the Nile Army. The government eventually decided to withdraw from the Sudan entirely, although Suakin remained an outpost of the Egyptian Army.

40 Major General Herbert Kitchener, Royal Engineers, 1885. At this time, he was an intelligence officer with the Gordon Relief Column. In 1892, at the early age of 42 he was appointed Commander-in-Chief of the Egyptian Army with the rank of Major General. In 1898 he commanded the Anglo-Egyptian forces in the Sudan and avenged the death of General Gordon at the Battle of Omdurman. He received the baton of a Field Marshal in 1909.

41 General Charles George Gordon, Governor General of the Sudan. Wearing the gold embroidered uniform of his office and the sash of the Order of the Nile. He died on 26th January 1885 at the fall of Khartoum, after a seige of 317 days. In the early hours on that fateful day the troops of the Mahdi had broken into the city and put everyone to the sword. Two days later the British relief force arrived by steamer, and on realizing that Gordon was dead the British troops reluctantly withdrew.

42 Tasso men Secret Society, West Africa, 1887. The society for men was called *Poro* which means law, but it is also a commonly used name for a vast and all powerful organisation whose dealings are conducted in complete secrecy. The power of the Poro was quite unrestricted and before its tribunal a person might be tried, executed and buried without the knowledge or agreement of the British administration. The wooden headresses are ornamented with human skulls and bones.

43 *Left* White hunter outside his tent, 1888. As ivory became more difficult to obtain, hunters became guides to exploration parties, and later guides to the rich big game hunters from Europe and America. This man has a pipe in his hand and a cup of tea at his elbow. The large bore double-barrelled rifle is capable of killing an elephant or rhino.

44 Prempheh I, King of Ashanti with his court, 1888. The third Ashanti War of 1893–94 led to the establishment of a British protectorate, and the fourth war 1895–96 ended with the capture of the capital Kumasi by Sir Francis Scott and King Prempheh was captured and exiled. The king was restored in 1925 and died in 1931. Nine other kingdoms made up the West African republic of Ghana as it is today, a member of the British Commonwealth since 1957.

45 Shot elephant and gun bearer, Kavirondo, near Lake Victoria, Kenya Colony, 1889. Elephants were numerous throughout Africa, but the trade in ivory decimated the large herds. Popular with the European hunters as trophies, the heads were mounted as wall decoration and the feet used for cigar boxes and umbrella stands. The hunter, Walter Bell, shot 210 elephants with a total haul of five tons of ivory in nine months.

46 Three shot elephants with gun bearers, Kavirondo District, Northern Kenya Colony, near Lake Victoria, 1889. Elephants live in herds and cause considerable destruction to the local flora by their eating habits. By the size of their tusks these particular animals are young and not particularly good trophies.

47 Lumbura tribesmen at a meeting with a British official, James Martin, 1889. He stands on the left with a pipe and an incongruous deerstalker hat. British administration tried to stop inter-tribal warfare, cattle rustling, and generally to keep law and order. They also acted as arbitrators in tribal and inter-tribal disputes.

35

48 Setting up camp on safari, East Africa, 1890. The tents are being set up, fires being made as the two white hunters look on. The tents are 7 feet × 7 feet with solid deal wood poles. The day's march will have been anything between 6 to 18 miles. If the local country is dangerous a *zariba* or fence of thorn would be cut and placed round the camp to keep out warring tribesmen, thieves, and animals.

49 Big game hunter with his gun bearer and headman, East Africa 1890. Skins are drying in the foreground and the hunter is holding antelopes' horns from an impala, which were found in large numbers from South Africa to the Sudan. The portable table at the back has the tea or coffee ready together with a bottle of whisky. It was the job of the gun bearer to clean and skin any game shot, as well as to look after the guns of the hunters.

21.

78.

50 *Left above* Crocodile hunting, East Africa 1890. The position of this hunter is very dangerous as a crocodile can move very fast for short distances over land. There are only two points on a crocodile that are immediately fatal: just behind the eye, or through the centre of the shoulder. The rifle most effective was a heavy .577. Crocodiles were to be found from the Nile to the south of Africa. A dangerous beast which often attacked the native population on the river banks.

51 *Left below* Hunter with his gun bearer and a rhino, 1890, East Africa. Found from Abyssinia down to the Cape in Victorian times, rhino were dangerous animals and would attack without provocation or reason. There were two species of rhino in Africa: the white rhino, and the black which was the most common. The specimen in this photograph is of the latter and has been killed by a shot to the heart.

52 Sir Frederick Jackson, with his trophy of an African buffalo, 1890. 'A savage animal when provoked especially when wounded. It has an intense fury and nothing will stop it except death. Should it succeed in overthrowing its antagonist it will not only gore its enemy with its horns, but will endeavour to tear it to pieces and will kneel upon the person and stamp it with its hooves, until the mutilated remains are disfigured beyond all recognition.' Jackson was a friend of Rider Haggard who later used him as a model for his character Goode in *King Solomon's Mines*.

53 Bringing stores to Johannesburg before the days of railway, 1890. A sixteen oxen team await the unloading of barrels. This was the most common mode of heavy goods transport in South Africa. The city of Johannesburg was founded in 1886 upon the discovery of gold. A 130-mile long reef runs through the district and has made the city larger and more commercially important than the capital of Transvaal, Pretoria.

54 Two married Zulu girls, *c.* 1890. The short skirt ornamented with beads and the tall headdress decorated with skewers of bone, are both signs of marriage. Unmarried girls wore their hair short and only a bead girdle. The calabashes, or pots, are used to carry home-made beer.

55 Suk warriors, Kenya, 1890. Their headdress is of ostrich feathers held into place by white clay which has been plastered to the head. As no clothing was worn there was a pocket in the headress for snuff, fire drills and beads. This tribe was to be found near Lake Baringo, which is to the north of Kenya Colony.

56 *Right* Natal native policemen, 1890. As law and order spread through the settlements, there was a need for native policemen to deal with their own people. A peaked cap and a blue tunic and trousers was all the uniform, as no boots were worn. A cane and a knobkerrie was the only armament. Other than a change of headdress the uniform was the same up to 1954. In the background stands a white policeman.

57 A group of Masai warriors, Kenya Colony, 1890. The Masai were a warlike tribe and each male had to serve a period of seven to ten years as a warrior, during which time he could not marry. The shield was made of ox or buffalo hide and quartered or designed in patterns of red, black and white. The headdress is made from a lion's mane. Spears, clubs and a sword were the usual weapons.

58 A group of missionaries on the West Coast, *c.* 1890. Many Christian missionaries had gone to Africa after Dr Livingstone had appealed to them to bring the blessing of Christianity to the African people. Wherever the British traders and hunters plied their trade, the missionaries were there also introducing the native people to the English language and helping to bring them into the twentieth century.

59 Rhodesian pioneers at the Nuanetsi River, 1890. When King Lobengula of Mashonaland signed over the mineral rights, Cecil Rhodes negotiated for about 200 pioneers to occupy the north of the country. They enlisted under semi-military discipline to colonise the country. They hoisted the flag at Port Salisbury on the 12th September 1890 after an arduous trek of over 400 miles across difficult country.

60 *Left* Slatin Pasha, 1895. An Austrian, Baron Rudolf Slatin, was Governor of Darfur Province in the Sudan for the Khedive of Egypt. At the time of the rising of the Mahdi, he held out with a few garrisons, but after the death of Hicks Pasha and his Egyptian Army, he was compelled to surrender in 1884. He remained in chains at Omdurman, but after ten years' imprisonment he managed to escape to join the British. He was attached to General Kitchener's intelligence service to identify and seize the Khalifa, after the Battle of Omdurman in 1895. He was successful but the Khalifa escaped, only to die in battle a few days later.

61 Cecil Rhodes in the Matoppos, on the site of his grave, 1897. Left to right: J. B. Williams Jerard; Hamilton Hall, an American mining engineer; Dr Thomas Smartt; Cecil Rhodes and a son of King Lobengula of Matebeleland. Writing to Jerard on 25th October 1927, Dr Smartt states, 'I think it was during this visit when one day Rhodes and I were alone, sitting on the granite boulders, he said he desired to be buried here.' Rhodes died in 1902 at the Cape, South Africa.

62 *Inset left* Privates Watts, Smith and McDonald of the Cameron Highlanders, after the Battle of Atbara, 8th April 1898. This battle ended in the defeat of Osman Digna, the Khalifa's lieutenant. These men are dressed in the new khaki uniforms, but with the kilt and sporran of a highland regiment. This regiment fought at the front of the British square and lost three officers and 57 men of other ranks. The Dervishes lost well over 2000. In the photograph can be seen some soldiers of the six Sudanese battalions who fought with extreme bravery in this battle.

63 First sight of the Dervish army 06.00 a.m., Battle of Omdurman, 6th September 1898. Three officers watch through binoculars as 8000 warriors, followed by an even larger mass of 20,000, head across the desert towards the British. At 06.25 a.m., at a range of 2700 yards, the Royal Artillery and the Egyptian Artillery opened fire. The battle had begun. It ended at 11.30 a.m. with 10,000 Dervishes dead on the field. General Kitchener and his army entered Omdurman later that afternoon. The death of Gordon was avenged.

64 First Battalion Grenadier Guards in action; Col. Hatton on his donkey, Omdurman 2nd September 1898. This battalion was the first to open fire on the Dervishes in section volleys, using the new Lee-Metford bolt action rifles that held a magazine containing ten rounds of ammunition. Few of the Dervishes got closer than 800 yards, and fought calmly and bravely. A British soldier remarked, 'those black chaps knew how to fight and how to die'.

65 *Overleaf* Dervish prisoners and Grenadier Guards, 1898. This picture was taken after the Battle of Omdurman, although the enemy do not look like the fierce fanatics depicted in pictures of the times. However, the fact that there were 10,000 dead and wounded in the battle gives some idea of its ferocity.

66 Sierra Leone Campaign, Fullah Mansah II and his Timani warriors, 1898. This was one of the small wars of British Colonial Africa, caused by a proposed tax scheme. The Mendi tribe, who had a reputation for a warlike nature, took advantage of the unrest to massacre their enemies and drive out the Europeans from the interior. They were eventually defeated by the army and frontier police. A number of chiefs remained loyal to the government and supplied auxiliary troops, and the photograph depicts these men whose knowledge of the country and native method of warfare proved invaluable.

67 *Right* Two hunters in a gorge on the Njoro River, Kenya Colony 1899. They are following the trail of waterbuck, whose head and horns were one of the chief prizes for an African hunter. They were once common along all of the East African territories from the Cape to Somalia. The hide made excellent shoe leather but the flesh was unpalatable to European taste.

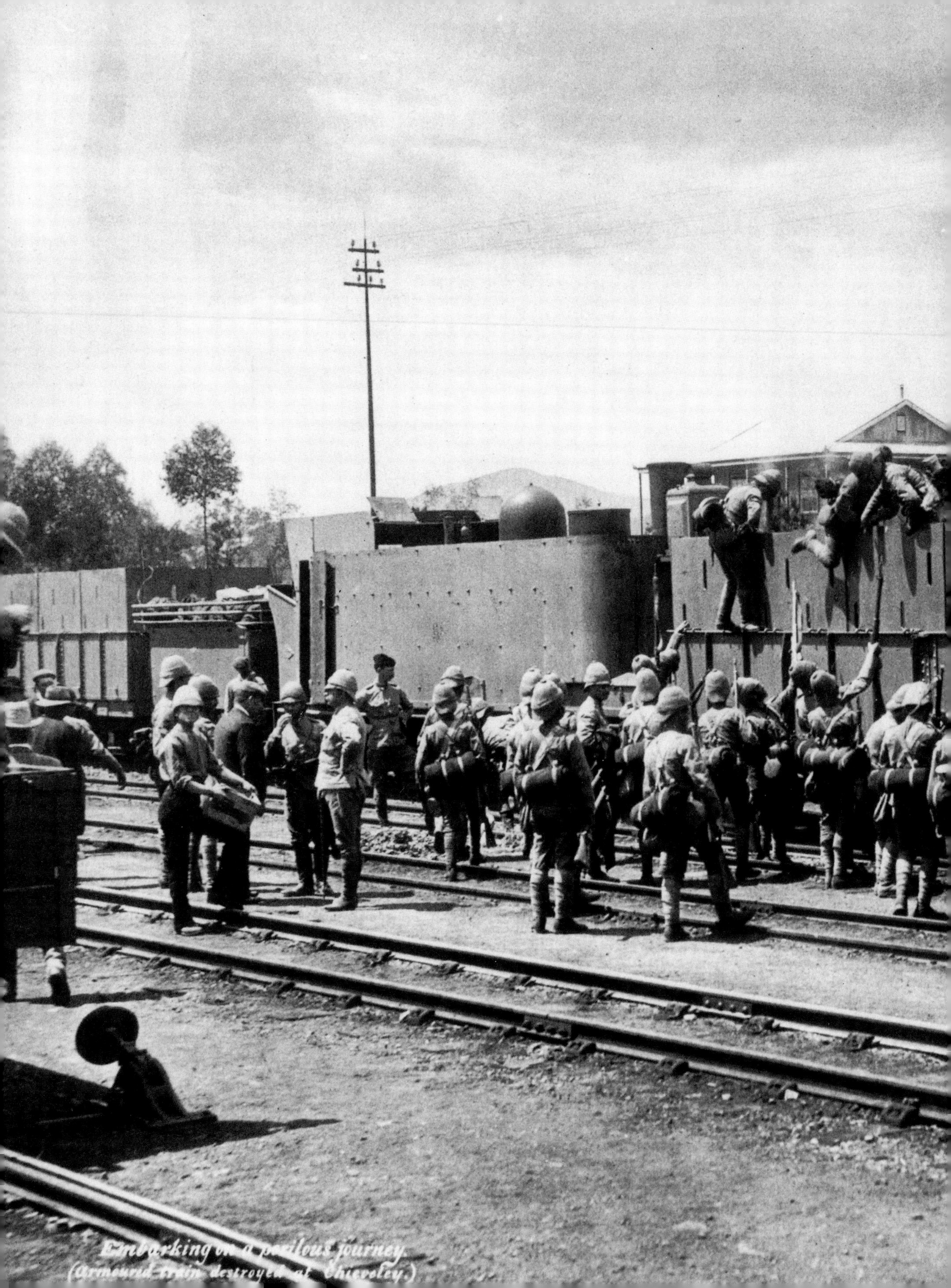

Embarking on a perilous journey.
(Armoured train destroyed at Chieveley.)

68 Second Battalion Royal Dublin Fusiliers embarking onto an armoured train, Boer War, 15 November 1899. The Boers blocked the line near Chieveley and lay in wait with a superior force, including two field guns and a maxim. Part of the train was derailed, and under a pitiless fire the men managed to clear the line. The engine on which the wounded had been placed got away, but left the rest of the men behind, and they were captured. These included Mr Winston Churchill, a newspaper correspondent, but on 14th January he managed to escape from Pretoria and rejoined the British Forces.

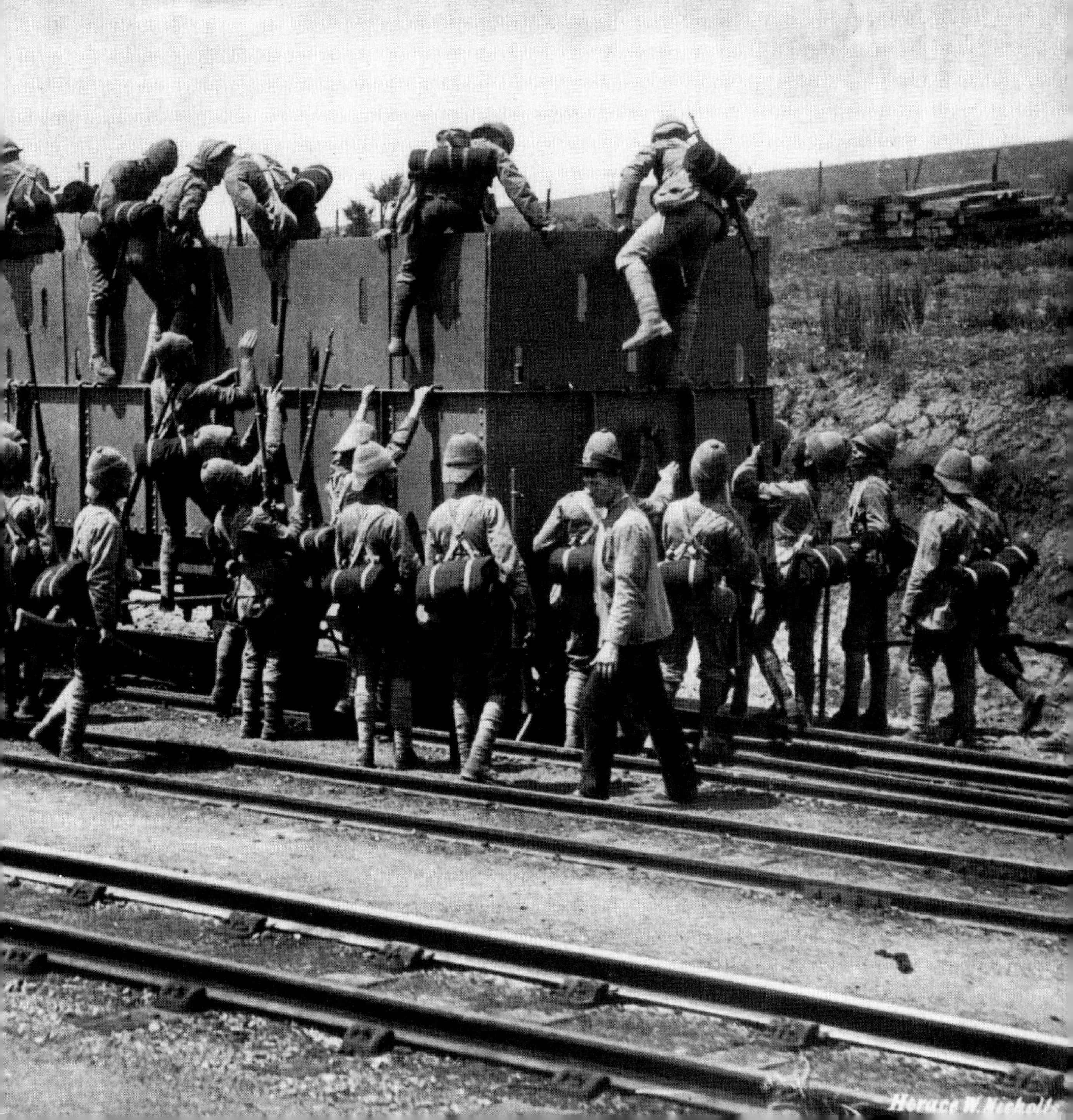

69 Cecil Rhodes at the seige of Kimberley, Boer War, 1899–1900. When General Cronje launched the war on the western front of South Africa he attacked Mafeking, while sending a second column against Kimberley, the diamond centre, near the Orange Free State border. The attack on 14th October turned into a seige, after the outnumbered garrison had fought off the Boers. Cecil Rhodes stands third from left. The town was relieved on 15 February 1900, having suffered 180 killed and wounded throughout the seige.

70 *Right* The crew of the colt machine gun, Boer War, 1900. This gun is mounted on a galloping carriage so that it can be rapidly moved on the battlefield. It was invented by the Earl of Dundonald, Colonel of the 2nd Life Guards, who received permission from the War Office to take out these carriages for trial at the front. As Lord Cochrane he was in Africa previously with the Nile expedition for the relief of Gordon, 1884–85, when he commanded the 2nd Life Guard detatchment of the Camel Corps.

71 *Left* A Field Officer of the Foot Guards ready to leave for South Africa, 1900. He is wearing the khaki service dress uniform with turned-down collar, brown leather buttons and Bedford cord breeches. The only distinguishing mark is the regimental flash on the left side of his pith helmet, which now has a plain leather chin-strap instead of the gilt brass chin chain. On his Sam Brown belt he carries a revolver and regimental sword in a plain leather scabbard. Brown leather gloves complete the outfit. This uniform, except for the headdress, was similar to that worn by officers in the First World War.

72 Royal Navy gun crew in action at the Siege of Ladysmith, 1900. The crew are sailors from H.M.S. *Powerful* and this gun is one of two brought up from Durban by Sir Hedworth Meux. Although the Boers bombarded the towns, the garrison fought off all attempts to penetrate the defences. After 119 days of siege, Ladysmith was relieved by an army under General Sir Redvers Buller on 28th February 1900. A total of 900 people died during this siege.

73 Military reconnaissance balloon in the South African War, 1900. It took four carts to carry the gas tubes and the equipment. Each was drawn by four horses, two extra carts were required to carry the baggage. The Royal Engineers balloon section had been in existence since 1890, and had previously been used experimentally in the campaigns of the Sudan and Bechuanaland. Three sections were dispatched to South Africa for artillery observations at Kimberley, Mafeking and Ladysmith. These balloons proved very successful in observing enemy movements, by direct telephone link.

74 Boer prisoners of war awaiting dispatch to a prison camp, 1900. By the time the war ended there were 40,000 prisoners. Some were sent to the island of Saint Helena in the South Atlantic and others further afield to Ceylon and Bermuda. The camps in South Africa itself were called concentration camps—a name that was to become notorious in the Second World War.

75 Lothians & Berwickshire Yeomanry, Boer War 1900. In response to the call for volunteers for this war, 5000 yeomen were formed into the Imperial Yeomanry for service in South Africa. This regiment was represented by five officers and 117 men and formed the 19th Company of the 6th Battalion Imperial Yeomanry. Their commanding officer was awarded the D.S.O. and the sergeant major the D.C.M. during the campaign. The regiment has its headquarters in Edinburgh.

76 *Right* Two men of the Imperial Yeomanry returning home from the South African War, 1902. In 1899, after the reverses suffered by the regular British Army, it was decided to send a volunteer force made up from the existing yeomanry regiments. At the first call for 5000 men the response was such that twice that number could have been despatched immediately. The terms for enlistment were for one year or not less than the duration of the war. There was also a grant of £65 to each man on volunteering. The slouch hat was very popular among these men, as also were gaiters instead of the tiresome puttees that had to be wound around the legs each time they were put on.

77 *Overleaf* Masai warriors at Miangi, East Africa, 1906. This tribe lived in the highlands of Kenya. Their favourite pastime other than raising cattle, was warfare. The British used them as auxiliary troops in native uprisings; since these were with tribes with whom they usually fought, this was greeted with enthusiasm, especially the capturing of enemy cattle, goats and women, in that order of precedence. In 1906 they were used by the British against the Nandi tribe who had been particularly troublesome, committing many murders and robberies.

78 Ex-American President Theodore (Teddy) Roosevelt during his African hunting trip of 1909. He stands with a magnificent specimen of rhino, one of 13 he shot on this trip. This fierce and dangerous animal fell 13 paces from Roosevelt's position. The rifle he carries is a Winchester model 1895, 405 calibre which was made especially for Roosevelt by the company. The game shot by the President's party totalled 152 animals—although some were collected for scientific reasons. Even during this period there were the first rumblings of game conservation, but little was done to stem the hunting of big game.

79 Woman dancer, Mendi land, Sierra Leone, 1910. One of the principal characteristics of the Mendi tribe was their love of music, singing and dancing. The costume consists of cotton over the body, long bushy bunches of palm fibre suspended from the wrists and arms, and small pieces of hollow iron attached to the legs for musical effect when dancing.

80 Two cannibal women from Sonkwala, Nigeria. Their necklaces are made from elephant hair, *c.* 1910. Cannibalism existed in many parts of West Africa. Sometimes the feast was a means by which to gain strength and courage before a battle. The Ganna-Warri tribe in the south liked the flesh because of the flavour, but usually it was a ceremony symbolic of gaining the attributes of a vanquished and brave foe.

81 *Right* A pair of ivory tusks at Zanzibar, 1910. These tusks were worth eighteen shillings per pound at this time. Ivory hunters had made great inroads into the vast elephant herds that covered Africa from the Cape up to the Lower Sudan. The trade in ivory was very profitable. This photograph was taken at Zanzibar on the east coast, the greatest port on that side of the continent for the export of ivory and slaves from the interior.

82 Girl from the Korama tribe, Nigeria, 1910. The metal rings on this girl's legs are her only clothing. Clothes were used solely as ornaments to dress up in on important occasions; but for everyday dress little or no clothing was worn, except perhaps oil on the skin. This girl is plaiting mats.

83 *Right* Bombari warriors, Upper Mendi, West Africa, 1910. These tribesmen are from the British colony of Sierra Leone and are armed with bows and arrows which were one of the more unusual weapons in West Africa. They also carry swords which had been introduced from the tribes of the Sahara desert to the north.

84 Pounding corn, Sierra Leone, 1910. The staff of life for many Africans was, and still is, grain, whether maize or millet, reduced to a pulp by careful grinding and bearing some resemblance to porridge. Cooking pots were brought to the fireplace and the maize and water boiled, usually only sufficient corn being ground for the consumption of one meal. Clotted milk was added or eaten as a separate dish. Game on the west coast was scarce by this time, except up country in the less populated areas.

85 *Right* Muganda warrior, 1910. His shoulders and legs are smeared with chalk. He is the champion warrior of his tribe and around his waist in battle was tied a rope by which he was restrained by other warriors, 'lest his courage should prove his ruin'. The shield is made of woven wicker strong enough to withstand a spear thrust.

86 On Safari, East Africa, 1910. The double tent was used to help withstand the great heat. Whilst the lady's hat is a little too fashionable for the African bush, the gentlemen look more the part in shooting jackets and pith helmets. The gentleman standing has a parrot on his wrist.

87 Accra Gold Coast, Fetish woman, 1911. The cotton skirt is a trade item made in Europe, but the beads and bracelets are made locally. Fetish comes from a Portuguese word 'feitico' which means amulet or charm, and because the Portuguese carried religious crosses and figures with them, the natives applied that name to all objects held sacred. The woman in the photograph looks after a shrine or object held in esteem by her tribe.

88 Transport in Kenya Colony, 1912. The lady and the little dog are sitting in a rickshaw introduced by the British. This type of carriage came from China and then spread to India, Japan, and Africa, where it was used in Cape Colony and Kenya, generally for hire as a taxi. Dress for gentlemen in the African cities consisted of a white linen or cotton suit with a white pith helmet, which would cost, at the time, £2 for the suit and 10 shillings (50p) for the helmet.

89 General Paul Von Lettow Vorbeck (*left*), German Commander in Chief, East Africa, 1914. During the First World War the British searched out the small German force in Africa in a game of fight and run. The general's aim was to hold out against a large allied force for as long as possible. This he did by fighting a series of skirmishes and battles until 1918 when he escaped over the Rovuma River into Portuguese Mozambique.

90 *Left* First Hertfordshire Yeomanry and the Bikanir Camel Corps in Egypt, 1915. They were both on a reconnaissance expedition in the Egyptian desert as far as Katia on the lookout for the Turkish enemy. Unlike the Western front, cavalry was an advantage in the deserts of the Middle East. Many of the Yeomanry regiments fought on this front, as did the Indian Army. The Bikanir Camel Corps was raised in 1884 and saw action in Egypt, Persia and Iraq during the First World War. The Corps was one of the state forces of his Highness the Maharajah of Bikanir.

91 German Askaris, 1914. The German Army in their East African Colony used and trained native Africans for their regiments. They fought extremely well under their German officers, and to the disappointment of the British, none of the native tribesmen rose up against the German colonists. They did, however, think that the British African troops sent from Nigeria and the Gold Coast would eat them.

92 Destroyed German gun, 1917. This is a 4.1 inch gun from the German cruiser *Konigsburg* and was abandond by the Germans when General Shepherd with the 2nd East Africa Brigade and the 2nd South Africa Brigade advanced to the Ruwo River on 21st March 1916. These guns were removed from the cruiser and mounted on wheels for mobility, after the cruiser had been put out of action as she lay on the Rufiji River.

93 Orderly cooks, Nigeria Brigade, at Dar es Salaam, 1917. This was the chief town of German East Africa and lay south of Zanzibar. The Indian Army proved susceptible to the fevers of Africa, which brought about an expansion of the African regiments, particularly from West Africa. These troops were well seasoned in fighting rigorous campaigns against slavers and hostile tribesmen in the sweltering heat of Nigeria and the Gold Coast.

94 Royal Garrison Artillery resting after a meal, 1917. The guns on the right of the photograph are limbered to motor trucks. This is a clearing in the bush and a meal has been consumed. Although this was a rigorous campaign in German East Africa, there appears to have been the comfort of tables and chairs for the officers seated on the left.

95 Buglers of the 3rd Battalion Nigeria Regiment, 1917. They are sounding the Hausa farewell. This was sounded off when officers and N.C.O.s left the country or were transported to other units. The pork pie cap is shaped similar to that of the Gurkha regiments but made of wool. The uniform was khaki, and consisted of shirt, shorts and putees, brown leather equipment with two pouches and their rifles. They would also carry on the campaign hatchets to cut their way through the dense jungle. Straw hats were also worn on occasions.

B.S.

96 *Left* Motor cycle dispatch rider on a bridge over the Runwu River, near Ruwu Top, May 1917. This is a B.S.A. motor cycle, and was extremely useful for delivering messages, or reconnoitring the enemy along the dense jungle paths. The soldier was unarmed and relied on his skill as a rider to get him out of trouble.

97 Wireless operators at Beho-Ju, German East Africa, January 1917. The wireless was a vital piece of equipment for the troops in the swamp and bush country of East Africa. The wireless set is on the left and in the centre is the generator which supplied the power. Gunnery was particularly controlled by this method, and in this campaign wireless observation from an aeroplane accounted for the destruction of the German cruiser *Konigsberg* as she lay hidden up the Rufiji River.

98 *Left* King's African Rifles on the march, January 1917. They are advancing along the right bank of the Rufiji River in German East Africa. The British attempt to invade the colony from the coast had been costly in terms of men killed by enemy machine gun fire, malaria and dysentry. The army pursued the Germans through the mangrove swamps and the bush until 1918, when the German commander Von Lettow Vorbeck escaped over the Portuguese border.

99 Packard lorry bogged down during rain on the Korogwe Morogoro line, 1917. The rainy season made the movement of transport a difficult task. Roads were non-existent anyway and the rain washed away any mud tracks there were. These trucks are of American manufacture and used to carry ammunitions or heavy supplies to the front line, which in Africa was always moving.

100 *Left* A village *Bundu* devil, Sierra Leone, 1920. There was generally a *Bundu* devil in any large village and her fetish power was very great. She would sit amongst a crowd of people and would enquire who was the perpetrator of some misdemeanour. The person to whom the twigs in her covered hands pointed to was killed or sold as a slave. The *Bundu* was a secret society for women, and the majority of women joined.

101 Coming of age ceremony of the Eliminya Society of South Kurkuruku, 1920. The initiation of young people into the tribe as men and women was an important ceremonial occasion and all African tribes practised some sort of initiation. At this ceremony tatoo marks were made and instructions in matters pertaining to marriage and tribal history were taught.

102 Nigerian girls, 1920. The bracelets are hippo ivory, the anklets are cowrie shells, and the necklaces, red beads. The occasion would be a tribal festival and the girls are dressed for dancing, as their normal day-to-day dress would be nothing at all.

103 Sudan horseman, 1920. This horseman is from the Baggara tribe. They hunted elephant for their ivory on horseback, and the people of southern Sudan for slaves. The long broad-bladed spear was a weapon typical of these people.

104 Arab girl of Zanzibar, 1920. The Arabs had been on the Island of Zanzibar since 1698 and it became a great trade centre for slaves and ivory from the interior of Africa. The Sultanate of Zanzibar came under British protection in 1890.

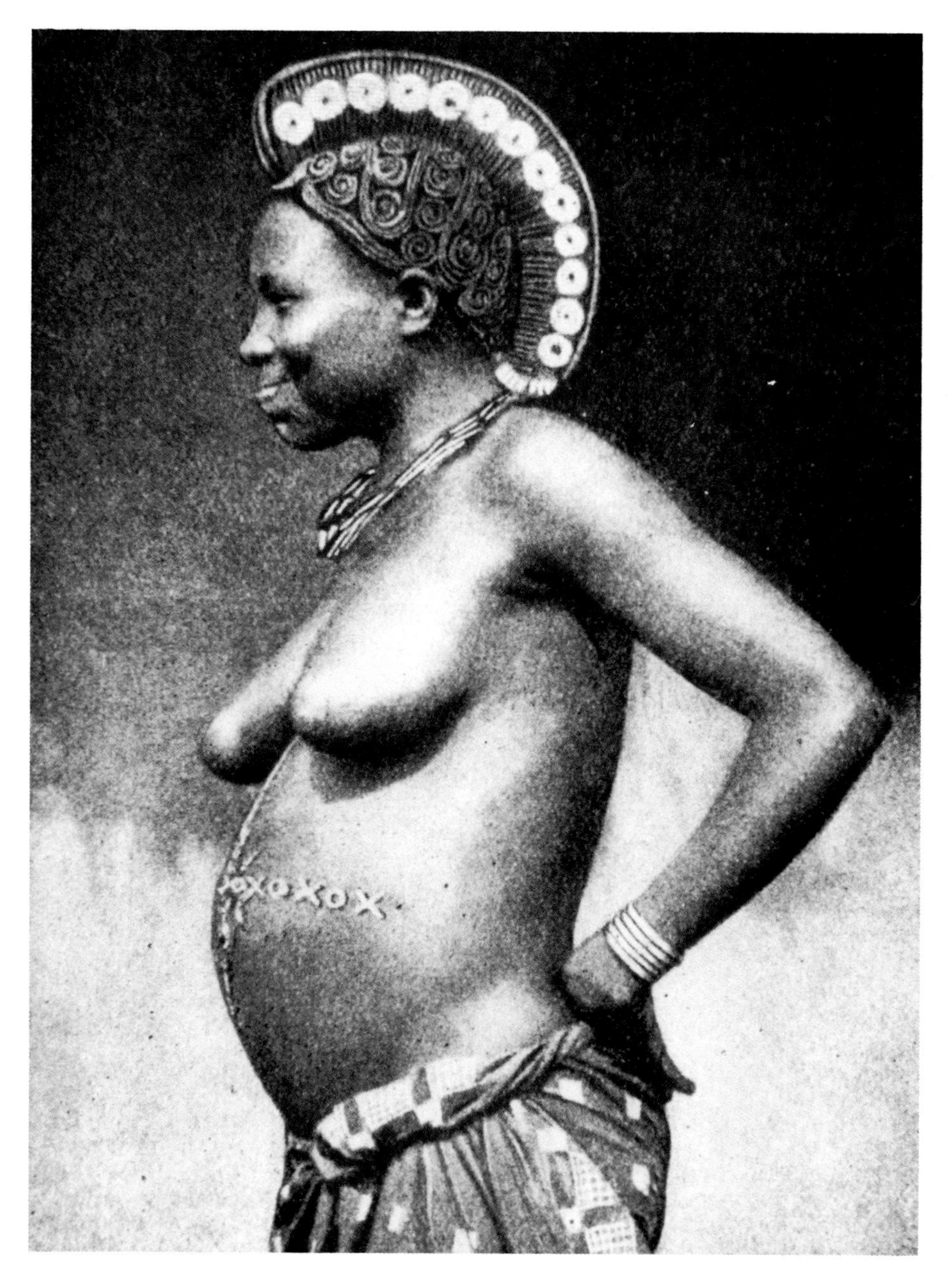

105 Awka woman, Nigeria, 1920. The crest is of wood ornamented with large pearl buttons over which the hair is combed, and it may not have been removed for some weeks, or even months. The scars across the woman's stomach are tribal marks produced by cicatrization.

106 Muhammadu Dikko, Ninth Emir of Katsina on a visit to England in 1921, with his brother. He was installed as Emir in 1906 and died in 1944 to be succeeded by the present ruler, his son Usman Nagogo. Katsina ranks ninth in order of precedence in the house of chiefs. Forty-nine emirates are included in the Republic of Nigeria—a member of the Commonwealth since 1960.

107 Sword bearer to the King of Bekwai, Gold Coast, 1924. The courts of the African kings had many ceremonial posts similar to those found in European courts. Apart from the sword bearer there would be the cup bearer, and of course the king's champion. The kingdoms of the west coast of Africa, through a long association with Europeans and their culture, had adopted some of their ceremonial ideas.

108 King of Bunyoro-Kitara (1882–1902). Twenty-fifth Mukama, Duhaga II was appointed ruler by the protectorate government in 1902. He was a staunch follower of the Anglican Church. He was succeeded by his half brother, Winyi IV in 1924. Four kingdoms are incorporated into the Republic of Uganda, which is a member of the British Commonwealth: Buganda, Bunyoro, Ankole and Toro.

109 King Archibong II of the Gambia, 1924. The trappings of royalty include a copy of the British Crown. The British were trading here since the eighteenth century and occupied a fortress at the mouth of the Gambia River. Trade thrived with Europe in gold, ivory and slaves.

110 Ovia dancer, Nigeria, 1925. Only men were members of this society. The prominent feature of his costume is the headdress of parrot feathers. The name is derived from a chief's wife, Ovia, who was hated by the other women. They caused her husband to quarrel with her and she turned into water. The ceremonies took place at the beginning of the dry season.

111 Sokoto horseman, northern Nigeria, 1925. The Sultan of Sokoto ranked first among the house of chiefs in Nigeria. The Sultanate dates from 1804 when the first Sultan laid the foundation of the Sokoto Caliphate and Fulani Empire. Feats of arms and horsemanship ranked high among these people. In 1903 the country came under British rule and influence, as with the whole of northern Nigeria.

112 A girl of the Shilluk tribe from the Sudan, 1925. These people inhabited the upper Nile regions, north of Uganda. The bracelets are of ivory, as large herds of elephants were always to be found in this area. The other jewellery is of brass and beads, and would have been bought in trade.

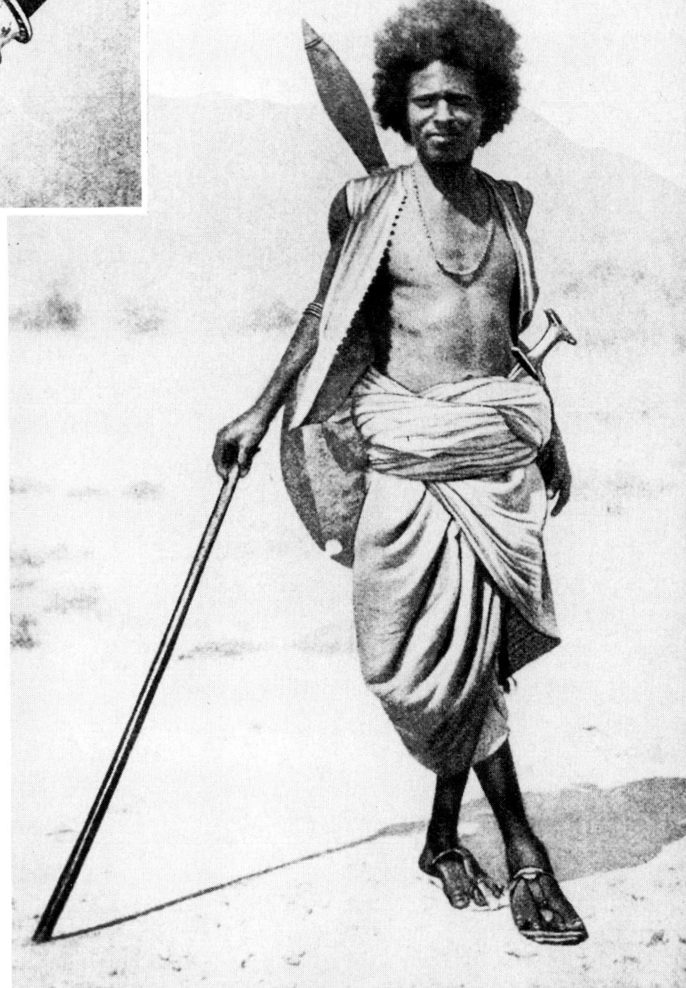

113 Hadendoa tribesman of the Sudan, 1925. These were the followers of the Mahdi and fought the British during the Sudan campaigns of the late nineteenth century. The shield is made of hippopotamus hide or crocodile skin. The sword has a straight blade with a cross hilt and is as sharp as a razor. In earlier times they hunted elephants armed only with their swords.

114 Gold Coast Fetish man, 1925. West Africa was rich in examples of sorcery and magic, despite the spread of Islam from the north of the country. Rites were performed by the people to placate evil spirits, ask for rain, or request success in a war. The forests were thought to be teeming with supernatural half-human beings, as well as ghosts of evil-doers. Ancestors were also worshipped, for those who did not have children became evil spirits. Human sacrifices were common, as was head-hunting on the west coast.

115 *Right* Woman of the Makonde tribe, Kenya, 1926. Small holes were made in the top lip in infancy and these were gradually enlarged until full-size discs could be inserted, usually of ivory. It is uncertain whether this custom of wearing lip discs originated through vanity or in an attempt to force slave traders to pass over the women.

116 Umar Sanda Kura, Tenth Shehu of Bornu, 1927. Bornu is one of the 49 emirates of Nigeria and ranks second in the house of chiefs. The Tenth Shehu died in 1937 at the age of 95 and was succeeded by his son, the present ruler. This family has ruled the state since 1846, which is in the north of Nigeria.

117 Hausa tribe women, 1930. The Hausa are essentially a nation of traders and their products were distributed over most of North Africa. Although they came from Central Sudan, the Hausa language became the trading language across central Africa, as far west as the Gambia. The religion of the Hausa was Islamic.

ACKNOWLEDGEMENTS

The author and publisher would like to thank the following for permission to reproduce photographs: The Victoria and Albert Museum: 1; The National Portrait Gallery: 2–4, 41; The BBC Hulton Picture Library: 5–7, 9, 11–13, 15, 26–7, 33–4, 37, 48–52, 54, 58, 61; The National Army Museum: 8, 14, 23–4, 36, 38–40, 65–6, 68–9; The Royal Commonwealth Institute: frontispiece, 10, 25, 42–7, 59, 62–4, 67, 77, 79, 81, 83–6, 88, 100; HM the Queen: 16–22, 35, 60; The Royal Anthropological Institute: 28–32, 53, 55–7, 80; The Imperial War Museum: 70, 73–5, 89–99; The Library of Congress (USA): 78. The author contributed photographs 71–2, 76, 82, 87, 101–17.